Decolonizing the Trinidadian Mind

With original poems and
select poems from the books
A Sliver of a Chance and
The Human Condition

Brian Sankarsingh

SG Productions

First Edition 2025

For permission requests, write to:
Sankarsingh Gonsalves Productions
c\o brian@sgproductions.ca

ISBN
Softcover - 978-1-7380419-8-5

History, Trinidad and Tobago
Colonialism

Contents

List of Illustrations

Foreword

History is not just a record of events; it is a living force that shapes our identities, influences our beliefs, and defines our future. In "Decolonizing the Trinidadian Mind," Brian Sankarsingh takes us on a journey from the arrival of the British in Trinidad in 1797 to our present-day republic, uncovering the deep psychological and cultural imprints left by colonial rule.

Sankarsingh and I grew up together in Trinidad before he migrated to Canada over 30 years ago. His journey has given him a unique vantage point, one that allows him to see our homeland both from within and from afar. As one of Canada's emerging literary voices and a Canadian Choice Award winner, he brings a depth of thought and a sharp analytical lens to this important work. His 2024 series, Enslaved, A Chronicle of Resistance also won the International Impact Book Award for Best Historical Fiction. Sankarsingh's writing is not just an exploration of history; it is a call to awareness, urging us to recognize the ways colonial structures still shape our society, our institutions, and even our self-perception.

In this book, Sankarsingh delves into the forces that have shaped Trinidad and Tobago's post-colonial reality, from the lingering effects of foreign governance to the ways our education system and cultural institutions still reflect colonial ideologies. He highlights the resilience of the Trinidadian people and the necessity of reclaiming an identity that is truly our own; one that is not defined by external narratives but by our own voices, stories, and aspirations.

Sankarsingh is a deep thinker, and his work challenges us to look beyond the surface of independence and examine the mental and societal shifts needed for true decolonization. His insights remind us that decolonization is not just about political sovereignty but also about psychological and cultural liberation.

This book is a crucial contribution to the ongoing conversation about our collective national identity. As you turn these pages, I encourage you to reflect on the past, question the present, and envision a future where Trinidadians fully embrace their heritage, free from the pressures and shadows of colonial influence.

Shrinivas Mohip

This book is dedicated to all the people who still struggle to break the yoke of colonialism. Your fight is our fight as we seek to create a kinder, safer world – Brian Sankarsingh

Introduction

The beautiful twin islands of Trinidad and Tobago have been called the paradise of the Caribbean. This treatise begins in a moment in the island's history that is pregnant with the weight of collective history and continues to an expectant urgency of the present. During this time, the people who have come to call the island home, bend – but are not broken - under this weight.

This therefore is the time to look back to a pivotal juncture that has shaped Trinidad and Tobago. We will travel back to an era marred by the brutality of British colonization, a time when the land echoed with the cries of enslaved Africans and the littered with the broken promises made to the East Indian indentured labourers from India. It is within this crucible of shared suffering and resilience that a Trinidadian identity was forged. This identity bears the indelible marks of a turbulent and sordid past. But this collective birthing pains, would result in the birth of a unique land and a special people. One where the African drums, would play in tune with the Indian tabla; where the sultry tones of the sitar intertwines with the steelpan, where AfroIndian dance and music would resonate with the heartbeat of the nation.

There are historical milestones that dot this landscape, but they are not mere relics of a bygone era. They are living testaments to the enduring legacy of oppression and resistance left by the British colonials.

From the sugar plantations that reeked of exploitation to the halls of power where political machinations continue to unfold, the journey from past to present is fraught with the echoes of triumphs and tribulations.

The narrative of Trinidad and Tobago is etched into our shared history with blood that runs deep. It is coloured with the hues of conquest and defiance, servitude, and liberation, but it retains its life-giving power.

Why, then, does history matter now, in this age that represents a dichotomy of progress and profound uncertainty?

The answer lies in the threads that bind the past to our present reality. Over the years, those threads have been woven into a tapestry of keen understanding that holds the key to navigating the complexities of our contemporary Trinidadian world.

Figure 1 - A Half-drawn picture of Trinidad via MS Designer

Those threads show the scars of colonization, the struggles for independence, and the quest for a new identity. They resound with a timeless relevance, offering insights into the challenges we face and the opportunities we must seize. This journey covers the tumultuous and rocky terrain that is Trinidadian history. However, together, we will try to understand and unravel the enigma of the past and by doing so hopefully illuminate a path forward.

I am a poet and author of Trinidadian descent; I encourage you to walk with me on this journey of self-discovery. We will stroll through a landscape rich with contradictions and complexities, where the echoes of history reverberate through the corridors to our present day. We will delve into the heart of our Trinidadian history. We will attempt to unravel the intricacies of the cruel and often ravenous forces that shaped our nation and tempered the resilience of our people. We will stroll through the labyrinthine power struggles and societal transformations that shaped our beautiful twin islands, shedding light on the interplay of religion, culture, politics, and identity.

Together, we will confront the ghosts of the past and the challenges of the present, seeking not only to understand but to reclaim the narrative of our history and the collective consciousness it has shaped.

This is not meant to be a historical account but a living testament to the resilience of our people, the complexities of our culture, and the indomitable spirit that continues to shape the destiny of our twin island paradise in the Caribbean.

The Arrival of the British

Sugar Cane Economy

Welcome to the tangled roots of Trinidad's history. Here the oppressive stain of exploitation and the shining opportunity of prosperity intertwine amongst the sugar cane stalks. This entangled chaos giving rise to a legacy that still shapes the island's identity today; and it begins in the boiling cauldron of colonialism and the sugar cane economy. This is where British and Spanish fortunes were forged, and the lives of our African and Indian ancestors were irrevocably entwined with the earth, air, and skies. But at this time, these Black and Brown lives had no worth other than the labour that could be wrung from every single muscle and sinew; and the colonial masters were ruthless when it came to profit. Over the years they had become extremely efficient at squeezing every drop of blood, sweat and tears from the people they colonized.

The earliest origins of Trinidad's sugar cane economy can be traced back to the 18th century when the island was transformed from a sleepy backwater into a hub of sugar and cocoa production. Although sugar cane was introduced to the island in the 1540s, it did not become the economic sugar behemoth for another 230 years [i]. Ah. Sugar cane. This amazing species of tall perennial grass with its sweet stringy stalks could be turned into sugar and alcohol. It was the European's insatiable demand for these commodities that fuelled the transformation of sugar cane planting, reaping, and processing. This was made more possible by Trinidad's fertile soil, and its tropical climate made it an ideal location for large-scale plantations.

This gluttonous demand led to the Spanish introducing African slaves to work the land. As the demand for sugar and cocoa grew, so did the number of plantations, and with them, the insidious institution of slavery took root, gouging itself into every fibre of the island's chemistry.

The following poem was written to help you think about that African enslaved man, up before dawn and toiling in the sugar cane fields late into the evening. He had no time or opportunity to search for a deeper meaning in life for his was one of endless brutal labour.

***

1. Thoughts of an African Slave in a Sugar Cane Field

I feel the sun beating down on meh back
But ah prefer that than to hear de whip crack

Ah been in dis field since before de sunrise
Oh gawd, ah go be here 'til de day ah dies

Nowhere to go, nowhere to run away
Dis where I am, and dis where I stay

Cutting de sugar cane, loading the cart
Massa ah tired, please have a heart

Buh Massa, he don't care if I am in pain
He only care dat ah cut dis damn sugar cane

Sometime ah feel I worth less than dis ting
All I really know is de sorrow it bring

***

The visual landscape of Trinidad was forever altered by the rise of these plantations. The verdant fields of sugarcane and cocoa trees stretched as far as the eye could see, a testament to the immense wealth that was extracted from the earth on the backs of these enslaved men and women toiling under an unforgiving tropical sun.

Ironically, if we shift our gaze to more modern interpretations and adaptations, we will still find that the echoes of the sugar cane economy thinking still reverberate through Trinidadian society. The legacy of exploitation and mistreatment has left a deep indelible mark on the collective consciousness. The modern-day descendants of those who once toiled in the fields continue to grapple with the weight and meaning of this history.

And yet, as with any chapter of history, there are challenges, controversies, and turning points. One of these turning points came with the abolition of slavery in the 19th century.

This marked a seismic shift in the island's trajectory. As it did in other parts of the world, this would shake the very foundations of the sugar cane economy. Indeed, it would subsequently give rise to another distinct flavour of slavery. Around 1845 [ii], a new wave of enslaved, under a new guise of slavery, began arriving on Trinidad's shores further shaping the island's cultural landscape. But more on that later.

Impact of Slavery

As we have discovered, Trinidadian history is intricately tied to the ruthless enslavement that once occurred on the island. That history is littered with pain, resistance, and enduring repercussions that continue to shape the Trinidadian society we know today.

We witness that resistance in the spiritual landscape though the obeah and voodoo rituals that still exists on the island today. It is also connected to the raw and sensual emotions that permeates Trinidad's Carnival.

Undoubtedly, the history of slavery in Trinidad is steeped in the brutal exploitation of African men, women, and children. These souls torn from their homes and forced into servitude; but it all began with that infamous Spanish explorer – who in this book, shall remain unnamed – and who led the exploitation of the indigenous peoples of Trinidad. He caused the population to be decimated by disease and destroyed through brutal subjugation. Those first indigenous people could not keep up with the cruelty and harshness that was meted out to them.

The demand for labour grew with the expansion of sugarcane plantations. The colonial masters needed their sugar fix. However, with the local population decimated the colonizers turned to African slaves. These Africans would eventually become the economic backbone of the burgeoning sugar, alcohol, and cocoa plantations as much as they were backbone of the cotton plantations in the United States. They became the human fuel that would be fed into the insatiable sugar cane economy's engine.

It was, therefore, the abolition of the Transatlantic Slave Trade in 1807 and the subsequent emancipation of all enslaved people in 1838 that marked that pivotal moment in Trinidad's history. Nevertheless, the legacy of slavery persisted; former slaves grappled with the harsh realities of their new-found freedom; enslavers continued their enslavement illegally [iii]. Into this volatile mix was added the East Indian indentured labourers. This only continued the marginalization, but this time instead of White superiority, it was shadeism. This is a phenomenon that was specifically curated by the British colonizers and used to their advantage among many of their colonies.

But let us revel in this post-emancipation period for a while. For it witnessed the emergence of vibrant African cultural expressions. Newly freed individuals sought to reclaim their identities and assert their spirit in the face of adversity. The echoes of their struggle reverberate through the pulsating rhythms of Carnival music. It lends its richness to the tapestry of Trinidadian folklore, and the speaks to enduring spirit of these people. From the pulsating rhythms of the steelpan to the colourful pageantry of Carnival, the fusion of African, Indian, European, and indigenous influences reflects the complex interplay of the island's shared and multi-storied history.

Meanwhile, the East Indians were wooed by promises of a three-year indentureship, the opportunity to earn a living and maybe even own land. Hundreds of thousands boarded ships bound for a land they did not know, to a future, the possibility of which only existed in their heads.

This poem was written from one such villager's perspective as he weighed the decision to leave his home in India and travel to Trinidad in search of a better life.

***

2. Colonial Indentureship

I'm a fighter, yes, and a survivor
I'll do anything it takes to live
Sure, I'm poor, but I am also provider
For my family all I have, I will give

The British have invaded my homeland
They've raped, plundered and killed
I lament and I pray for our children
Prabhu[1], will we ever rebuild

[1] Prabhu means master or prince in Sanskrit and many of the Indian languages; it is a name sometimes applied to God.

Hunger grinds and rips in my belly
I'm sure I will soon be dead
Then a visit by a man from Delhi
Has left me with dreams in my head

"Leave your village and come away with me!"
Said the man as he told me his plan
"To a place, far away, and o'er the sea
Forge your future in a wonderful new land"

"There you'd have a better tomorrow
A chance at a brand-new life
A place without so much sorrow
A place without hunger or strife"

A place where I could earn a living
In the field planting sugar cane
I was unsure, I had my misgivings
But I had nothing to lose. Lots to gain
As I step on the gangplank I wonder
"Is this my biggest mistake"
With the chance of a much brighter future
It was one, I was willing to make

***

In the modern context, the legacy of slavery continues to manifest in many ways. The enduring socio-economic disparities, the struggle for racial equality, the hate that was encouraged between the races by the colonizers, and the ongoing quest for justice underscore its enduring impact. Yet, even here, in the darkened shadows of our past, with the interplay of the racial tensions between Blacks and East Indians, there is a glimmer of hope – a growing consciousness among many, that seeks to confront historical injustices and instead foster a more inclusive and equitable society.

However, that enduring spectre of colonialism and slavery does not go away easily. The debate over reparations, the reclamation of cultural heritage, the need for forging stronger ties between Blacks and the East Indian diasporas pose profound challenges that demand a collective reckoning. As Trinidadian society navigates the complexities of its colonial history, its people must continue to push for dialogue and embrace the transformative power of discourse, debate and understanding. This can begin from a place of shared suffering under the colonial yoke, but it must progress to a place of collective hope and shared optimism. Unfortunately, however, the impact of colonialization on the Trinidadian mind continues to insert its way into the conversation, pitting Black brother against East Indian brother.

Much as we may want to ignore it, the truth remains that the legacy of slavery and indentureship and the consequent manipulation by the colonial masters are scars etched upon our collective Black and Brown Trinidadian souls. Those scars can remind us of the pain, hate, poverty, and destituteness of the people. It is only through empathy, conversation, and the willingness to understand that we can decolonize the Trinidadian mind and tap into the enduring strength and resilience that defines us as a nation.

The sad and terrible reality though is that we are also the ones that will allow hate and pain to cause divisiveness, disagreement and continued racial hate between our two races. This was how the colonial masters divided and conquered their colonies and this still exists.

In the end, in this present moment, as it was in the past, we must choose the path we wish to take: one of discord, disharmony and hatred or one of congruence, racial harmony and unity.

Slave Revolts

In the shadows of the Caribbean's untamed beauty, a tempest brewed. Tension hung in the air, and the soil seemed to stir with the restless spirits of those who dared to defy the chains that bound them. Here under the scorching sun, in the sugarcane fields came whispers of pain as the plantations groaned under the weight of human suffering.

Do not be fooled by the lush greenery and azure skies, for the cruel dance of oppression is playing out. The setting is one of stark contrasts - the immoral opulence of the colonial estates juxtaposed against the abject misery of the enslaved populace. It is within this cauldron of inequality where man's inhumanity to man was laid unabashedly bare that the sparks of rebellion would ignite.

In our narrative, the main players emerge from the shadows; their names are etched in the foundation of resistance. They are not mere pawns in the grand chess game of history, but souls who dared to defy the status quo. The enigmatic historian C.L.R. James [iv] wrote about them.

People like Toussaint L'Ouverture [v], whom James called the Black Spartacus. He was born a slave, but he led one of the largest and most successful slave rebellions in history. Or strong women like Queen Nanny, also known as Nanny of the Maroons [vi]. She was the leader of a community of formerly enslaved Africans. They were called the Windward Maroons. These people's stories are woven into the stories that tell of the struggle for freedom. Each tale of resistance stands as testament to the resilience and indomitable spirit.

It has become chic to ask how the African enslaved were kept enslaved for so many centuries. Why didn't they resist?

Well, they did.

They fought against their enslavers with every fibre of their being.

The following poem is not a condemnation but reflects the reality of a system of thinking that once existed and the tendrils of which still permeate and contaminate societies around the world.

***

3. The Burden of Colour

Oh animal, without purpose, your destiny
Is to be in all manner of sin
Oh animal, I do this to save you
From the beast that lurks within□

The chains that rankle around your neck
Are there for your protection□
Without your master's firm embrace
You will have no direction

The whip you feel upon your back
Hurts me more than it hurts you
Having to damage my property
Is not something I lightly do!

But animal you won't understand
This is beyond your comprehension
What use is this kind of punishment
If not to stop your further dissension

God, He, has granted me
This holiest dominion
Borne upon my pale white skin
With His divine recognition
But you, oh animal of mine
With your skin of varying colour
Subjugation is your lot
To be forever in my power

My fellowmen, we all agree
There are levels of being human
And though you may oft look like me
You're still what we call sub-human

My god's promise of saving grace
Oh, animal it's not yours to claim
Yet serve me well and you'll endure
A minimum of pain

But do me wrong, and you will face
The righteousness of my anger
There will be no place for you to hide
From my accusing finger

So, go back to your place in line
Equity is not an ambition
Next time you raise it you'll feel
Much more than my admonition

***

The core challenge that pulsates at the heart of this narrative is one of oppression and conversely, the unyielding quest for liberation. It is the historical equivalent of the irresistible force encountering the immovable object.

The enslaved Africans throughout the Caribbean, stripped of their humanity and shackled by the chains of servitude, stood face to face with the formidable might of their oppressors.

Figure 2- Haitian Revolution - Public Domain

The struggle for freedom was not merely physical but also a battle for the very essence of their being. It was a fight for dignity, for the right to exist as more than mere chattel.

In the face of such overwhelming odds, the approach taken by the enslaved Africans was one of unyielding defiance. From clandestine meetings under the cover of night to whispered promises of solidarity, they forged a network of resistance. Their methods were as diverse as they were audacious, from acts of sabotage to open revolt, each a resounding declaration of their refusal to be subjugated.

The results of their daring efforts echo down the corridors of time to our present day. These small, yet significant, reverberations of resistance would not only shake the very pillars of the colonial edifice but also sow the seeds of future liberation movements. Their impact was profound, their legacy enduring.

The story that emerges from this tale of defiance is one of hardiness and the unyielding spirit of the human soul. It is a testament to the enduring quest for freedom, a quest that transcends the boundaries of time and place.

The slave revolts in Trinidad and Tobago are not mere isolated incidents but threads in the rich tapestry of human history, each a reminder of the unquenchable thirst for liberty.

We do well to honour people like Sandy [vii], an enslaved African who led the first major revolt in Tobago in 1770. Under his leadership he was able to provide such resistance that the British were forced to bring battleships from Grenada.

As we consider the legacy of the enslaved Africans and their daring revolts, we are compelled to ask:

What echoes of their struggle reverberate in our world today?

How can we honour their memory and carry forward the torch of liberation?

These questions linger like the fading echoes of a distant drumbeat. They invite us to continue our march deeper down the corridors of history.

Shadeism, The Legacy of Slavery

Have you ever wondered what might have been going through the mind of an enslaved person? From the moment they were forced into a ship's hold to the first sting of the whip on their back. What looked like a "better life" to them? What changed in their minds as they grew to understand the reality of the situation, they had found themselves in?

This poem contemplates the mix of emotions that they may have felt. As you read it keep in mind that this person's identity until now would have been as part of a tribe. The entire tribe was a unit where each person had a place.

***

4. No Sojourn

I feel the sting of the master's whip
The contempt in his voice for my race
Pray that I'd never be an absconder
Else bring to my master, disgrace

He says that I'm much less than human
That I could not cope with the weight
He's sure I'd rather be beaten
Treated like a lesser primate

I should, he says, be glad for the favour
Of stealing me from my homelands
There I'd surely be in more danger
Of the beasts that roam my grasslands

When he whips me, he shows me no mercy
He's the master and I am the slave
I am lesser, than even the Comanche
This is what I must take to the grave

He builds fortunes on the back of my labour
Gilded luxuries are what he has earned
Me, I am just an invader
For me, today there will be no sojourn

***

Within the intricate fabric of Trinidadian culture and identity, the enduring legacies of slavery and indentureship are threads that weave through each life. It is a legacy that is at once both haunting and illuminating. It plays a part in shaping our society, our values, and our understanding of self and neighbour in profound and complex ways.
The slave trade brought a steady influx of African captives to the shores of Trinidad, where they were subjected to unimaginable brutality and exploitation. The sugar plantations, with their insatiable demand for cheap labour, became the epicenter of this inhumanity.

The eventual abolition of slavery in 1834 represented a watershed moment in Trinidad's history, marking the end of one form of bondage. Unfortunately, it also heralded the dawn of a new era of struggle and adaptation for the newly freed population.

That legacy of slavery, however, did not vanish with the stroke of a pen; it continued to linger and fester in the hearts and minds of the descendants of the enslaved. It distorted and often misshaped their worldview, and this informed their place in Trinidadian society.

They were free, but they had nothing. For years of gruelling labour, back breaking toil under an unforgiving Caribbean sun, they had nothing to show for it.

Their oppressors, however, continued to feed off the fat of the land.

Figure 3- Sugar Cane - Henri Georgi (Vers 1853-1891) - Centre des archives d'outre-mer Public Domain

Undoubtedly, the legacy of slavery manifests differently across cultures and communities in Trinidad. The Afro-Trinidadian experience, with its deep roots in the trauma of enslavement, is undeniably distinct from the indentureship legacy of the East Indian community.

Yet, in the crucible of our shared history, these two legacies are inextricably interwoven. Sadly, it is here, that the colonial masters saw an opportunity to divide and rule. These seeds of division would lead to turbulent and tumultuous times. Unfortunately, this divisiveness continues to haunt and split Trinidadian society to this day. Black against Indian reverberates throughout history. It is heard in children rhymes; it is seen in the ongoing struggles for social justice; the struggle for economic empowerment, and cultural recognition and as we will see later, even crime and political corruption.

The reclamation of African heritage and identity has become a powerful force in Trinidadian music, art, literature, and activism. It provides a vital counterpoint to the erasures and distortions of history that have sought to diminish the significance of the enslaved experience.

However, the enduring impact of systemic racism, economic inequality, and social marginalization continues to cast a long shadow over the Trinidadian landscape. It constantly reminds us that the scars of slavery run deeper than mere historical memory. The racism perpetuated by the colonial masters between the Africans and East Indians also continues to exist. This bizarre racism of colour has had its proponents on both sides of the racial divide.

When confronted with these challenges, we are called to reckon with the enduring legacy of slavery in all its forms and all its complexity. We must in turn acknowledge the pain and suffering of our ancestors on both sides of the racial spectrum. It is only then that we can bring honour to their resilience and resistance in the face of unimaginable adversity shared by both Black and Brown.

***

5. Divide and Rule

He whispers "You're much better than them,
They were all born as slaves
As Indian you are a part of the realm
Those people don't even have names"
In hushed tones he says to the Black man
"Indians feel they're better than you
They say you're worse than a caveman
Don't trust Muslim or Hindu"

Now as the Black and the Indian fight
Hate brewing heavily on both sides
Much to the colonial master's delight
They're easier to rule if they divide

Oh but my people that time has long past
Yet still we hate as they taught us
Who would think that such a thing would last
And would continue to haunt us.

***

We must force ourselves to remember that the legacy of slavery and indentureship in Trinidadian culture is – first and foremost a story of triumph over tragedy for both races.

Figure 4 - Definition of Shadeism

It is also one of resilience in the face of oppression and subjugation. It is the story of the enduring power of the human spirit to transcend great hardship. It is a story that continues to unfold, shaping our understanding of self and society, and challenging us to confront the legacies of the past with courage and compassion.

As we contemplate the complexities of our shared history, we cannot allow ourselves to forget the indomitable spirit of those who came before us. After all, it is their legacy that lives on in the rhythms of our hearts and the contours of our souls.
Black and Brown peoples must learn to embrace this legacy, with all its pain and in all its beauty. We must learn to recognize the thread of colonial manipulation and acknowledge what it has done to us. We must open our minds to learn of the history of our fellow Black and Brown people. Understanding that, helps us to contextualize actions and reactions. Only then, can we really begin to understand what it means to truly be Trinidadian. Only then can we begin to decolonize the Trinidadian mind.

Abolition of Slavery

As we noted previously, the abolition of slavery marked a pivotal moment in the collective TrinBagonian[2] narrative. It heralded the dawn of a new era while casting long, haunting shadows that ominously linger in the recesses of our national consciousness.

6. Freedom

Freedom!
I have longed for it from birth

[2] A colloquial compounding of Trinidadian and Tobagonian

Sinews straining against chains
I feel the call of Mother Earth
Going through freedom's birth pains

Freedom!
Enslavement it all that I know
Freedom, a thing for which I yearned
This is a transformation I must undergo
Pray that I will emerge unburned

Freedom.
Blood, sweat and tears on the sugar cane
Callous hands and bowed back
Oh child, how can I ever explain
What it means in this world to be Black
Freedom?
Now what must I do to survive
I must find a way on my own
Do what I must to remain alive
At least in this thing I am not alone

***

The timeline of the abolition of slavery in Trinidad is punctuated by significant milestones, each marking a small victory in the arduous struggle for freedom. From the formation of abolitionist movements to the passage of legislative acts, the journey towards emancipation was filled with adversity and resistance.

The Emancipation Act of 1833, set the stage for the eventual freedom of all slaves in the British Empire. It stands as a watershed moment in our collective history, signaling the beginning of the end of this abhorrent practice.

Figure 5 - Breaking free - Public Domain

With the stroke of a pen, the chains that bound our ancestors were shattered; yet it is essential to recognize that the abolition of slavery unfolded differently across various regions, each grappling with its unique set of challenges and triumphs. In Trinidad, the fusion of African, Indian, and Indigenous cultures in the wake of emancipation began to evolve into a rich amalgamation of traditions and customs that continue to shape our national identity.

However, there was a darker, more sinister side to this as well. The tragedy of the old colonial trick of dividing and conquering. This happened as soon as the East Indian indentured labourers disembarked from the ships that brought them from the continent. They were told that they were "different" than the newly freed African slaves. In that "difference" many of them heard the word "better." They, after all, would be earning their living and they had the opportunity to purchase land after their indentureship. Meanwhile, the whispers in the ears of the newly freed Africans were that these people were here to take whatever opportunity they could. This could be viewed as hostile for a newly freed enslaved African, who had nothing and whose only means of earning an income was to sell his labour to the same sugar cane plantations that forced him into slavery in the first place. Pitting the races against each other also meant lower labour costs for the plantation owner.

Undoubtedly for the African, this journey towards emancipation was not devoid of challenges and controversies. The transition from slavery to freedom forced the newly liberated individuals to grapple with the daunting task of forging a new identity in a society marred by deep-seated inequalities. These inequalities were exacerbated by the division that was fostered between the Africans and newly arrived indentured East Indians.

This holdover, this despicable legacy of slavery and colonization, cast a long shadow, perpetuating systemic injustices. The struggle for true emancipation, for a true decolonizing of the Trinidadian mind continues to this day. It remains an evolving narrative that demands our unwavering attention, understanding and empathy.

In the wake of the abolition of slavery, Trinidadian society faced a crossroads; a juncture where the collective psyche bore the scars of oppression while hearts and minds yearned for a brighter future. The abolition of slavery was not just a legal decree; it was a seismic shift in consciousness which in some ways represented an awakening to the inherent dignity and rights of every individual, regardless of their race, background, or circumstance. It was a clarion call to build a society on the principles of equity and justice.

We must acknowledge that the abolition of slavery was not merely a chapter of our collective our history. It was the genesis of a profound reclamation of shared humanity, a declaration that no chains, whether physical or metaphorical, can ever shackle the indomitable Trinidadian spirit.

Figure 6 - A picture of a ship full sails

Indentured Labour

In the history of Trinidad and Tobago, the story of the indentured labourer is a complex, and intriguing narrative.

Whilst we can never understand the many reasons why our East Indian ancestors decided to leave their homeland; we are grateful that they did.

The sugar cane fields sway in the Caribbean breeze, with their verdant leaves softly whispering untold secrets of the enslaved Africans and their fight for freedom. That freedom was now at hand and brought with it a host of new problems. At this time there was a call for labour that echoed far and wide. It crossed the oceans, reaching the distant shores of India. The

promise of a new beginning, a chance to escape the shadows of poverty, or even escape one's caste. The call lured thousands of Indian men, women, and children to embark on a journey to a land unknown, a land called Trinidad and Tobago.
This poem imagines the story the British colonial masters may have told the villager to sell him on the idea of indentureship.

***

7. Indentured - Part I

Come, come away with me, to a land of milk and honey
A place to stake your claim
A land of opportunity
Your honour to reclaim

Come, Come and join me, in this brand-new land
A place to call your very own
This beautiful island
Is an ideal steppingstone

Think not about the voyage
Across the ocean blue
It is but an annoyance
To your personal breakthrough

Slaves will never be your name
Indentured labourer you will be
This is not even the same
Come with me and you will see

Come, come away with me, to an island in the sun
Your King will so be grateful
To each and every one
His indulgence will be faithful

Come, come away with me, on this adventure grand
Making a way, where there is none
Come help us tend this land
Under the bright Caribbean sun

***

In 1845 the first ship left the Indian continent with a ragtag group of East Indians. They were heading to the Caribbean to work on the sugar plantations. The abolishment of slavery inspired a new type of ownership – being indentured by debt to the British colonial empire that ruled their continent.

Within the shackles of servitude, it seemed that the East Indians saw the possibility of a new and better life.

Figure 7 - Indentured labourer cutting cane with buffalo in the background – Public domain

8. Trinidad

I stand and stare in wonder at the sight before my eyes
If anyone had said it was real, I'd swear their words were lies
It could carry hundreds of elephants, and not sink to the depths
A ship so large, so overpowering, it takes away my breath

"Be prepared," I heard someone yell, "for a journey across the seas"
"Come with all that you have, but there'll be no need for rupees"
I've packed my cloves and ginger, mustard, spices, ghee
I even brought some peppers and mangoes for my chutney
They've banned the owning of slaves, so I go to a place called Trinidad
In my dreams, it's as beautiful as Delhi, as mysterious as Hyderabad
Three years is the commitment, then I'd be free to leave
If I work hard, and save my coin, there is nothing I can't achieve

Fath Al Razak
Alnwrick Castle
Allanshaw, and
Grecian, too
Brenda
Avoca, and
Clyde
Mutla
Chenab, and
Rhone
Hereford

Jarawar, and finally, the Wiltshire

All packed with human beings
Some chasing their own dreams, others were just fleeing
Lord Shiva, help me, please, don't let me die in this place
I'm seasick with the to and fro, and we're packed tightly in this space
We're not allowed up on the deck; there's no sunshine or fresh air
The captain and his sailors say, we'd be much better off down here
Why did I ever want to leave; now hunger doesn't seem so bad
I'd rather go back and face my fate; I promise to God I'd be glad
When will it end, this torturous trip? My days melt into each other
I want my feet back on dry land; I cannot go any further
"Land ho, Land ho!" I hear the shout, amid the breaking waves
Could it be true, I have escaped the jaws of a watery grave
We pile out of that dreaded ship's hold, with all our earthly possessions

There's no time for sights and sounds, just time for circumspection
"Name!" shouts the Englishman "Naam kya hai?" he screams
Shankar Singh I reply, almost woodenly, as if woken from a dream
"Sankarsingh, put your thumb print here—you need to get to work
And after you're finished with me, go see that other clerk"
And so, begins my three-year stay in this strangely familiar place
I'll do my work and save my coin and make it by God's grace
I work in the sugar cane fields, cutting cane well into the night
Then stumble home to my hut, with the help of a small lamplight
Days they come and then they go; soon my three years are all done
But this place is now my home, with my wife, daughter, and son
I will not be going back; Trinidad is my new land
Here is the place I'll survive and thrive; here is the place I will make my stand

***

At the heart of this story stand the indentured labourers, their faces etched with determination, their souls burdened with the weight of uncertainty. These resilient souls, willingly uprooted themselves from their homeland, carrying with them the traditions, music, food, languages, and dreams in a small bundle on their back. Their arrival reshaped the cultural fabric of Trinidad and Tobago, infusing it with the melodious songs, euphonious language, and vibrant hues of their East Indian heritage.

Furthermore, it is important to understand what it truly meant to willingly cross the ocean[viii]. It was forbidden to willingly cross **kala pani** translated as the black water. Crossing the seas to foreign lands would cause the loss of a person's social respectability. It would also lead to the putrefaction of their cultural character and negatively affect their posterity. There was also the idea that crossing the ocean meant that reincarnation cycle of the person would end. This was because the traveler would be cut off from the regenerating waters of the Ganges.

Unfortunately, even the abolition of slavery had not taught the colonial masters any lessons in equality. For the indentured labourers, the core challenge lay in the exploitation and subjugation. A colonial bait and switch. Upon disembarkation, they found themselves bound by contracts that often-resembled chains of servitude. The promise of a better life was often overshadowed by the harsh realities of labour under the scorching sun, the cramped quarters of the barracks, and the callousness of overseers.

The promise of breaking the cycle of poverty was mercilessly reneged on and there was no going back. Yet, amidst the adversity, the Indian diaspora found solace in the bonds of their community. They sought refuge in the embrace of their cultural and religious traditions, their food, and their music. The effect of these things can be seen, tasted, and heard in the almost every aspect of life in Trinidad and Tobago to this day.

They were known as coolies, a word that initially meant unskilled labourer but that would eventually come to be used as a vile derogatory racist term. For the indentured labourer it would become as distasteful to hear that word, much as the recently freed African hated the "n-word." This was not lost on the colonial masters who used every means at their disposal to ensure that the Indians and Africans did not unite. They knew that such a thing would mean an immediate loss of control of the island and its rich resources.

***

9. Reinvention

I am not who I once was
There I was Dalit[3], lower than the low
Here I could be anything no one would ever know

Here, I can reinvent myself
There I had no future, no opportunity
Here I can make a new life in this community

I will be what I want to be
Stopped only by the weariness in my bones
Here I decide my future, me, and me alone

***

The legacy of indentured labour endures in every facet of daily life in Trinidad and Tobago. Their tireless work in the cane and cocoa fields, laid the groundwork for the flourishing agricultural landscape, while their

[3] Dalit, also previously known as untouchables, is the lowest stratum of the castes in the Indian subcontinent.

indomitable spirit sowed the seeds of an Indian community that continues to thrive.

As we reflect on this chapter of our twin islands' history, we cannot ignore the shadows of racism and bigotry that linger born in the past that continues to grow today. They would be used to poison the water that flowed between the African and Indian communities. Those scars of indenture run deep. They leave us to think about the moral and ethical implications of treating humans – because of their skin colour, race, or creed – as lesser than human. This racism will have enduring impact on the collective psyche of the nation.

Imagine a sepia-toned photograph capturing the stoic visages of indentured labourers toiling in the fields, their sweat-soaked brow a testament to their unwavering perseverance. This poignant image serves as a stark reminder of the sacrifices made in the name of progress.

Figure 8 - East Indians in Trinidad - Public Domain

The narrative of the Trinidadian indentured labourer intertwines with the overarching theme of colonial exploitation and is undoubtedly interwoven into the exploitation of the Trinidadian African enslaved. To deny this connection would be to deny reality. These brutal acts of colonization sheds light on the interconnectedness of global histories and the enduring legacy of imperialism. They are a poignant reminder of the depths of depravity to which some people willingly sink.

Conversely however, they also show the resilience of the human spirit in the face of adversity and their enduring quest for dignity, justice, and freedom.

Cultural Mosaic

In the tapestry of Trinidadian identity, threads of history, tradition, and migration are intricately woven, forming a vibrant and diverse cultural mosaic. This fusion of African and Indian influences birthed a unique identity. It is a living testament to the resilience and creativity of a people shaped by their collective history and the uncomfortable bond of racism, shadeism, cruelty and oppression that was used to bind them together.

Trinidad's cultural landscape reflects the island's complex history of colonization, slavery, and indentureship. The fusion of African and Indian cultures has played a pivotal role in shaping the island's identity. It has given rise to a dynamic and multifaceted society.

The arrival of Indian indentured labourers, after the African enslaved were freed, planted the seeds of this cultural amalgamation that would redefine the island's social, cultural, and racial fabric. The mid-19th century marked the beginning of this transformative period, as the Emancipation of African slaves in 1838 and the arrival of Indian indentured labourers in 1845 set the stage for a dynamic interplay of traditions. The blending of African and Indian customs, languages, music, and cuisine flourished in the vibrant melting pot of Trinidadian society, creating a unique cultural synthesis that transcended boundaries.

Imagine a canvas alive with the vibrant hues of carnival celebrations, infused with the pulsing and rhythmic beats of African drums and the melodious strains of Indian tabla drums. This visual feast captures, this ubiquitous melding of diverse cultures captures the essence of Trinidad's cultural mosaic. It is in this magical place that every brushstroke tells a story of resilience in the face of oppression, adaptation despite unsurmountable odds, and unity despite colonial conspiracies.

***

10. Black and Brown

I am Brown and you are Black
But should colour have any impact
On how we survive and live together
After all we shared an oppressor

Should we not have learned the lesson
That nothing good comes from oppression
Why must there be a superior race
When we have all suffered in this place

In the face of the White man's slavery
You fought with exceptional bravery
We were duped by indenture's lie
But we both chose not to comply

We've more in common than you might think
We should work together and not be hoodwinked
Colonization rules through causing division
But together we can choose a better vision

A society where we live in harmony
Rising above petty racial controversy
Black and Brown together as one
Celebrating under the Caribbean sun.

***

In contemporary Trinidadian society, the cultural mosaic continues to evolve, embracing modern interpretations and adaptations that reflect the island's ongoing journey of self-discovery. From the emergence of new musical genres that blend African and Indian rhythms to the fusion of culinary traditions in a dynamic gastronomic scene, the spirit of cultural synthesis remains a driving force in shaping the island's collective identity.

Figure 9 - African and Indian drums MS Designer

However, this cultural fusion has not been without its challenges. The legacy of colonialism and the struggle for cultural autonomy have led to complex debates involving race, culture and belonging. Yet, these moments of tension have also become turning points, sparking conversations that delve into the nuances of identity and belonging. As these conversations continue to evolve, we can only hope that they will ultimately enrich the cultural mosaic with a deeper understanding of its complexities and richness.

In the poem Indentured Part I we read about how the East Indian was persuaded and coaxed into travelling to an unknown land in search of opportunity. The man who speaks to him in Part I, like any snake oil salesman, sells him a beautiful dream of reinvention of self and the endless opportunity.

Part II is the reality of what the indentured labourer faced when he arrived on the island. The dream becomes a nightmare from which there is no escape.

***

11. Indentured - Part II

Now that you're here, one thing to know
You're still subjects of the King
And on him you must bestow
Your life and everything

The sugar cane waits for no man
The next three years you're mine
Welcome to new Hindustan
Do the work that you're assigned

Work, work, and work some more
Do this for your King and country
One day you'll have your crore[4]
But first you pay your bounty

There's no such thing as going back
You still owe us for the journey
You'd better get yourself on track
Or we'll run out of mercy

In this land you have no dominion
This truth you'll take to your grave
Here the Empire is sole sovereign
And you its indentured slave

***

In this ever-changing landscape, the Trinidadian cultural mosaic stands as a testament to the enduring spirit of resilience and creativity. However, even in this place, it must evolve, and the fact remains that to evolve to the next best version of themselves, Trinidadians must address the profound questions of identity and heritage.

---

[4] An East Indian unit of measurement, esp. money

These are not questions about East Indian indentured labourers or freed African slaves. They even go beyond being questions that pertain to Afro and Indo Trinidadians. They are questions about what it means to be Trinidadian.

The answer to these questions offers a future that is a mesmerizing array of colours and patterns, each fragment contributing to the breathtaking whole. It can be a future that is a living, breathing testament to the power of diversity and the art of cultural synthesis.

One that invites us to celebrate the boundless possibilities that arise when we truly allow the rich and diverse cultures and traditions of the people to intertwine and flourish.

Struggle for Independence

Nationalist Movements

The quest for independence and self-determination encapsulated in the debate of nationhood wove a vivid narrative that shaped the essence of Trinidadian politics and society.

These seeds of Trinidadian nationalism were sown in the fertile soil of adversity. They were watered by the sweat and tears of generations yearning for autonomy from the colonial stranglehold. The island's history bears witness to a struggle that transcends mere political upheaval; it is an unyielding quest for self-discovery and empowerment.

The earliest origins of nationalist sentiment can be traced back to the sugar cane and cocoa fields where both the enslaved Africans and indentured Indians toiled. The land, knowing the blood, sweat and tears of each race, heaved as both races hungered for true freedom from the colonial masters.

This fusion of African, Indian, and Indigenous influences birthed a unique ethos, sparking a fervent and inimitable desire for self-governance. The fires of resistance were kindled in the hearts of those who refused to be mere pawns in the grand chessboard of colonial dominion. This nascent yearning for autonomy laid the foundation for the monumental movements that would emerge in the years to come. In the early 20th century, the vibrant voice of Trinidadian nationalism found resonance in the articulate rhetoric of the nation's leaders.

Figure 10 - Upraised fist against colonization - via MS Designer

Arthur Andrew Cipriani [ix], a White Trinidadian man, served as mayor of Port of Spain, and was elected member of the Legislative Council. He served as leader of the Trinidad Workingmen's Association (TWA) and founder of the Trinidad Labour Party. His impassioned advocacy for the rights of the working class ignited a spark that would ignite the flames of self-determination. He would eventually be called the pioneer of the nationalist movement in Trinidad.

Tubal Uriah Buzz Butler [x] was originally an immigrant from the island of Grenada, led labour riots in 1937 which resulted in the formation of the modern Trade Union movement.

Dr. Rudranath Capildeo [xi] who studied law in London and was admitted to practice as a Barrister-at-Law in Trinidad and Tobago in 1958 founded and led the Democratic Labour Party from 1960-1969.

But it was Dr. Eric Williams [xii], whose impassioned vision galvanized the masses. This marked a turning point in the struggle for autonomy. The winds of change gathered momentum and Dr. Williams' clarion call for a united Trinidad and Tobago struck a resounding chord with those yearning for liberation.

The crowning glory of this trajectory was the attainment of independence in 1962. This was a watershed moment that heralded a new dawn for Trinidad and Tobago. The tireless efforts of leaders such as Dr. Williams and Dr. Rudranath Capildeo paved the way for a sovereign nation, free from the yoke of colonial rule.

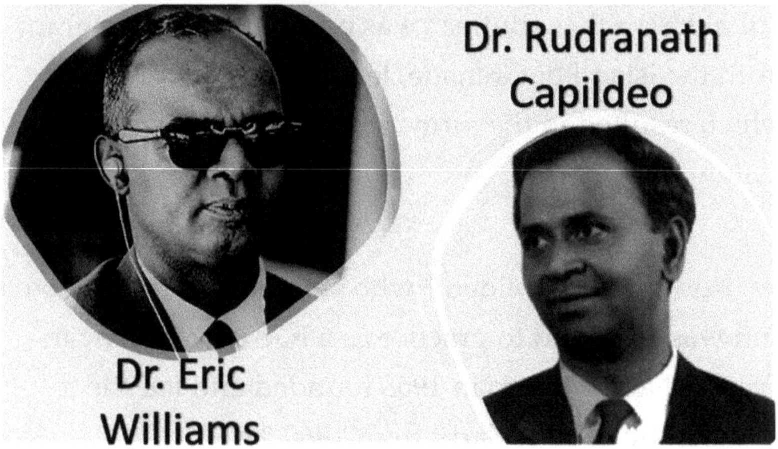

Figure 11 - Dr Eric Williams and Dr. Rudranath Capildeo

The evolution of nationalist sentiments in Trinidad bore the rich hues of cultural and regional diversity. The Afro-Trinidadian, Indo-Trinidadian, and other ethnic communities each contributed their distinctive brushstrokes to the vibrant canvas of the nationalist struggle.

The quest for self-determination has evolved into a dynamic dialogue, embracing new paradigms of inclusivity and social justice.

***

12. My Trinidad

This is my Trinidad
My ancestors blood and sweat
Permeates the ground
My nation under the sun
To this picturesque land
My eternal soul is bound

This is my Trinidad
My roots are planted deep
In the hills and valleys of this land
From Port-of-Spain to Cedros
We delight in the pleasures of
Our beaches and sun-kissed sand

This is our Trinidad with
Its callaloo and crab or
Doubles and curry chicken
Saltfish buljol, bake and shark
Black pudding, oil down and souse
Every dish is finger licking

This is our Trinidad
Standing together as a people
We can achieve our hearts desire
We can break the chains
Of colonialism and be
Forged in liberty's fire

***

Trinidad's journey towards independence was not without its challenges and thorns, controversies, and pivotal turning points. The struggle for autonomy unearthed deep-seated fissures of racial prejudice and religious intolerance that tested the resilience of the Trinidadian spirit. Unfortunately, many learned the game of division from the colonial masters well. Quite early on encampments were built based on those racial and religious differences.

The quest for unity amid this divisiveness continues to shape the contours of Trinidadian nationalism in the 21st century.

Colonial Oppression

The history of Trinidad is a story of conquest and resistance, of the clash between imperial ambition and the fierce will of a people yearning for autonomy. It is a story of white supremacy, colonial imperialism, and racism. In the beginning, the nefarious shadow of colonial oppression loomed large over the island. It cast a long and sinister silhouette on the collective consciousness of its inhabitants.

The seeds of this colonial oppression were sown in the in the collective minds and hearts of Trinidad. Like a relentless tide, the Spanish, Dutch, and French vied for dominance, each leaving their mark on the island's language, cultural and political landscape. However, it was the iron grip of British colonial rule that would come to define the era of oppression that followed.

The Treaty of Amiens in 1802, officially ceded Trinidad to Britain. This was a significant blow to Spain for at that time Trinidad was their colony. The British Empire wielded its power with ruthless efficiency and did not hesitate to establish plantation economies.

The Hosay Massacre of 1884 stand as a testament to the simmering discontent that pervaded the island. On 30th October 1884, a procession of some 6,000 Muslims was fired upon by British troops. The legacy of colonial oppression manifested differently across Trinidadian society, with the diverse cultural fabric of the island lending unique hues to this struggle for liberation. The East Indian indentured labourers, the African descendants of enslaved peoples, and the indigenous Amerindian communities each bore the weight of oppression in their own distinct ways, shaping their collective identity and resilience.

In the wake of independence in 1962, Trinidad embarked on a journey of self-discovery, seeking to reclaim its multicultural heritage and assert its autonomy on the world stage. But the scars of colonial oppression continued to influence the island's social, economic, and political landscape, serving as a poignant reminder of the enduring impact of this historical trauma. Sadly, even today, this specter of colonial oppression continues to cast a long shadow over Trinidadian society, as the scars of the past intersect with the complexities of the present.

That colonial oppression permeated the Trinidadian air. Its rancid stench made its way into many African and Indian minds and hearts. There it simmered and bubbled, biding its time, and deepening its roots. The colonials had used race to divide and rule through the Legislative Council. Playing one race off against the other was, however, only one course. Amongst the East Indians they also drove religious wedges between the Hindus and Muslims. Given the penchant for enmity between them, this was not difficult to do, but it was done anyway.

***

13. Sowing Divisiveness

Your passport is the colour of your skin
Fairer, like the White man, is preferred
Thus, it should be without and within

This shall always be – you can rest assured

Light skin we will countenance in the public eye
Though we know it sets brother against brother
We know that hate will toxify
And spill over to include all others

A whisper here, a favour there that is all we need
This is how we rule all our colonies
As you fight, we sow dissension seeds
For this we make no apologies

Black against Brown, we can surely do that
We can even set Muslims against Hindus
We can even pit caste against caste
Don't ever bet against us, you'll always lose

You see colonized people are already filled with hate
And all we do is stoke the fire
There is no need for us to destroy or decimate
That is how we built this great Empire

***

Path to Independence

Given all the colonial interplay behind the scenes, the story of Trinidad and Tobago's path to independence can be viewed as a saga of triumph over adversity. This pivotal moment arrived in 1956 when the People's National Movement (PNM), under the leadership of Dr. Eric Williams, won the general elections. This marked the beginning of a new chapter in the nation's history, as the call for self-governance grew louder and more insistent.

In 1962, the dream of independence became a reality as Trinidad and Tobago shed the vestiges of colonial rule and emerged as a sovereign nation, proudly hoisting its own flag, and charting a course towards a future. This flag, designed by Carlisle Chang, was chosen by the independence committee of 1962. The colours of red, black, and white symbolized fire (the sun which represented courage), earth (representing dedication) and water (which represented purity and equality).

This flag was a powerful visual aid that symbolized a period of transition and the dawn of a new era. The path to independence was not easy or straight. The legacy of colonialism cast a long shadow, leaving behind racism, divisiveness, social and economic disparities that continue to shape the nation's trajectory. Inevitably, this struggle for true independence went beyond the mere trappings of statehood. The decolonization of the Trinidadian mind would remain an ongoing endeavor and Trinidad and Tobago continues to grapple with what it means. It adds nuance to the already existing challenge of nation-building in a rapidly changing world.

***

14. Paradise

They speak about the cascadura fish[5]
And what happens when you eat it
But I think there is more it this
Whether you choose or not to believe it

Trinidad and Tobago can be paradise
Twin islands bathed by the sun
If we can only shift the paradigm
And be a united nation

Casting aside racism and hate
Thinking only of our beautiful land
If everyone can learn to advocate
For peace amidst the sea, sun, and sand

Oh, what a country we could build
Starting with peace and love in the centre
Our national destiny fulfilled
And be rid of the colonial tormentor

***

[5] The legend of the cascadura fish made popular in a poem written by Allister Macmillan that says "Those who east the cascadura will, the native legend says, Wheresoever they may wander, end in Trinidad their days"

Figure 12 - A cascadura fish - Public domain

Post-Independence Challenges

On that day in 1962, as the sun rose on the dawn of Trinidad and Tobago's independence, the nation stood at a crossroads. This was a juncture where the dreams of a people collided with the harsh realities of statehood. The jubilation of freeing the country from colonial rule was palpable. It ignited a fervent hope for a future of autonomy and, hopefully, prosperity. Yet, as the fog of euphoria disappeared in the heat of reality's sunshine, it unveiled a landscape filled with challenges and obstacles. It presented a terrain that demanded resilience, ingenuity, and unwavering devotion to building the nation and engaging all its people.

The post-independence era ushered in a time of profound transformation for Trinidad and Tobago. The nation, which was once tethered to the whims of its colonial masters, now grappled with the weighty responsibility of self-governance. However, this newfound freedom was accompanied by a host of formidable hurdles that threatened to ensnare the nascent nation in a tangle of uncertainty and discord. Establishing a cohesive national identity was extremely important.

For centuries, the yoke of colonialism had left its imprint on the collective consciousness. It twisted and shaped perceptions, values, and aspirations to serve the needs of the empire. Now as the shackles of imperialism fell away, a void emerged. The question of what it truly meant to be Trinidadian despite race, colour, or creed. What did true nationhood mean? How could the new fledging nation embrace its rich tapestry of cultures and traditions and weave it to form a cohesive whole? Was this even possible? The answers to these questions were the most pressing concern.

***

15. Free

Free!
  We free from the yoke of colonialism
  Tie 'round we neck for so long
  Sick of all the imperial sophism
  With their unbearable dance and song

Free!
  We finally free to build we own nation
  Ready to take our place in de world
  Here we go build ah Trinidadian foundation
  With the red, white, and black flag unfurled

Free!
  We responsible for we own destiny
  Leading the way for the region
  Creating a unique Trinidadian legacy
  Together in unity and cohesion

Free!
  To create we own thing
  In our variety, we can find similarity
  Blending, mixing, intermingling
  For today and for posterity

***

In the crucible of post-independence Trinidad and Tobago, the forging of a cohesive national identity emerged as an imperative. It was a journey that required the nation to embark on a voyage of self-discovery, unearthing the treasures of its past and breathing life into the aspirations of its future.

The echoes of history reverberated as the people of Trinidad and Tobago stood poised to write a new chapter of independence and nationhood.

Here they could sculpt an identity that would stand as a testament to their resilience and unity. This new Trinidadian identity could sound a beacon that would illuminate the path for future generations.

The consequences of failing to address this fundamental challenge would be dire. It would mean a fragmented culture where it would be easy for anyone to sow seeds of discord and division. A fragile society where fracturing the newly minted unity would hamper progress and possibly destroy the nation. Without a cohesive national identity, Trinidad and Tobago risked being adrift in the Caribbean Sea.

Creating a flag that told the story of the island's strength was a first and crucial step. Carlisle Chang designed the flag that would serve as a profound symbol of this identity. A national anthem that would resonate with people from all social classes was another important foundational element. Patrick Castagne wrote the lyrics of the anthem –

Forged from the love of liberty
In the fires of hope and prayer
With boundless faith in our destiny
We solemnly declare:
Side by side we stand
Islands of the blue Caribbean Sea
This our native land
We pledge our lives to thee
Here every creed and race find an equal place
And may God bless our nation
Here every creed and race find an equal place
And may God bless our nation

A national motto that spoke about the need for unity was next. Dr. Eric Williams, who was the first Prime Minister to hold office after the country became independent proposed "Together We Aspire, Together We Achieve."

To surmount this challenge, all these essential symbols of nationhood were needed. However, what was more important was that the nation needed its leaders to begin weaving the disparate threads of its cultural mosaic into a tapestry of national pride and unity. It needed its leaders in Government and Opposition to develop a strategy that would celebrate diversity while fostering a shared sense of belonging. Leaders who could paint a picture that would resonate with every Trinidadian heart, regardless of creed, colour, or class. This had to be done through words and actions! If political leaders could inspire this spirit of togetherness and belonging, then community leaders among the people would take up the standard.

Of course, there were alternative solutions. Leaders could pursue the assimilation or imposition of a singular cultural identity. However, going down that path, they risked erasing the unique tapestry of Trinidad and Tobago's cultural landscape, stifling the many beautiful and diverse voices that – up to this point – had marked the nation's identity. Embracing diversity as a source of strength, rather than seeking homogeneity, proved to be the best path forward.

Formation of Republic

August 01st 1976, marked another significant milestone in the history of Trinidad and Tobago and its transition from an independent colony to a republic. This symbolized a momentous step to full sovereignty and true self-governance for the nation. The journey towards republic status had profound implications for the political, social, and cultural fabric. Although the penultimate end of this journey happened in 1976, it was truly rooted in the country's colonial past.

The decision to transition to a republic was not abrupt but rather a culmination of evolving national identity and aspirations. The Republican Constitution of Trinidad and Tobago was crafted through extensive deliberation and consultation with various stakeholders, reflecting the nation's desire for self-determination and autonomy.

One of the defining features of the newly minted republic was the replacement of the monarch, through her representative, the Governor General (GG). The GG was replaced with a President, elected for a 5-year term by all members of the House of Representatives and the Senate plus Speakers from both chambers. Furthermore, the transition to a republic necessitated amendments to the nation's constitution, outlining the roles and responsibilities of the President, the Executive, Legislature, and Judiciary. These changes reinforced democratic principles and institutionalized the separation of powers.

Embracing republicanism served to strengthen Trinidad and Tobago's sense of national identity and unity. This transition marked a significant assertion of Trinidad and Tobago's sovereignty and independence on the world stage. It provided an opportunity for the nation to redefine its relationships with former colonial powers and assert its place among the community of nations.

Despite the change in political structure, Trinidad and Tobago's transition to a republic ensured continuity and stability in governance. The institutions established during the colonial era evolved to adapt to the new republican framework, to maintain stability and continuity in the functioning of the state. What was not anticipated was that these institutions would carry on with a colonial mentality even as they embraced the nation's new sovereignty.

Legacy of Colonialism Redux

It is undeniable that, even with the creation of the Republic, the echoes of the historical trauma of colonialism reverberate through the social, economic, and political fabric of the people of Trinidad and Tobago.

The roots of British colonialism in Trinidad and Tobago can be traced back to the 16th century. The islands were coveted by many European powers because of its sugar cane and cocoa. The British empire was allured by its fertile soil, abundant resources, and strategic positioning in the Caribbean. The island came into its own as a British colony, however this stage for a tumultuous journey marked by exploitation, violence, and cultural upheaval.

The arrival of the British in the late 18th century ushered in a new era for Trinidad and Tobago. The imposition of plantation economies, the transatlantic slave trade, and the reshaping of land ownership all heralded an era of profound transformation. Furthermore, after emancipation, the legacy of indentureship left its own mark on the people's collective psyche. Later, the struggle for independence, and the complexities of post-colonial governance all played their own roles in driving wedges between the people. Eric Williams coined the phrase "Massa Day Done" as a clarion call to the population to change their thinking. The word massa was a shortened form of Master. The enslaved were not allowed to call their enslavers by their names, thus Master became Massa. What Williams was speaking about here was a different mindset.

***

16. Massa Day Done?

Massa day no more,

We shed the trapping of the monarchy
This 'aint no time, like it was before
We no longer want that autocracy

Massa day, finally done
We free to run the country as we please
One people under the sun
We feel the embrace of the Caribbean breeze

But how do we really break the chains
That we have borne for generations
How do we free ourselves from the constrains
How can we truly take back our nation

The oppressive stench of colonialism
Revisits our lives at every turn
How do we break free from that cabalism
Before we reach a point of no return

***

This legacy however is not a monolithic force; it subtly weaves itself through the cultural and regional aspects of Trinidadian life, with nuanced intricacy. The fusion of African, Indian, Chinese, and Indigenous influences bears the unmistakable stamp of colonial encounters. Each bear scars and wounds that affect their

Trinidadian identity and ultimately how they interact with each other.

Contemporarily, the legacy of British colonialism continues to manifest in subtle yet pervasive ways. We see this in the subtle but enduring influence of British legal and educational systems, the echoes of colonial mentality in societal structures, and the bitter fruits of the seeds of racism that were planted so many centuries ago.

The tendrils of the past continue to intertwine with the present. These scars of exploitation also left an uneven distribution of wealth among certain races. This too had an enduring impact on the interaction between races.

We cannot deny that the echoes of the past continue to reverberate through the present. However, if we can identify and address these complexities of colonial legacy, we have an opportunity to change the Trinidadian mind.

The Current State

The Politics of Ethnicity

The politics of ethnicity or ethnic politics is an ever-present force in Trinidadian. This term is not merely a convenient label; it encapsulates the complex interplay of identity, power, and allegiance that has affected nation's political landscape since the earliest post-colonial days.

At its core, ethnic politics refers to the influence of ethnic identity on political behavior and decision-making. It is a simple yet potent concept that holds within it the seeds of both unity and division, cooperation, and conflict. In a country as diverse as Trinidad and Tobago, where the colours of our heritage paint a vibrating mosaic, the impact of ethnic politics muddies and distorts every facet of our collective existence.

Key to understanding ethnic politics is recognizing the profound significance of ethnic identity itself. Our ancestry, traditions, and cultural heritage are intricately woven into the fabric of our being, shaping our values, beliefs, and perspectives. When these identities intersect with the realm of politics, they give rise to a complex interplay of alliances and rivalries, aspirations, and grievances.

For example, the nation's Hindu population saw the need to establish an organization that would advocate for, and give voice to, their people. The Sanathan Dharma Maha Sabha (SDMS) is one of the largest and most influential organizations in Trinidad. It was formed in 1952 by Bhadase Sagan Maraj who facilitated the merging of several other organizations. This consolidation was effective in creating a cohesive and singular voice for many of the nation's Hindus. Maraj would go on to play a founding role in several political parties and organizations.

The historical and etymological context of ethnic politics in Trinidad and Tobago traces back to the legacy of colonialism and the dynamics of power and privilege that it fostered. Our history bears the indelible imprint of colonial rule, which not only sought to exploit and subjugate but also deliberately engineered divisions along ethnic lines to consolidate its authority – a "Divide and Conquer" approach. This legacy remains a blot on the current divisive political landscape. It provides structure and improperly shapes the narratives of race, equity, financial acumen, and other dynamics that define the present reality.

***

17. We are Trinidadian

Indian must support Indian and
Who to ketch, ketch
African supporting African
Leaving the Dougla like a wretch
But what if there is a better way
To help our nation advance
What if we could find a way
Would you take the chance?
Can we forget past injustices
Or stop judging people by race
Can we sit together and discuss this
Without spiralling into racial hate

Although it may be our cultural heritage
Is not about African and Indian
It is more than just our parentage
The fact is WE ARE ALL TRINIDADIAN

***

To contextualize ethnic politics within a broader framework, we must acknowledge its pervasive influence on governance, policymaking, and the distribution of resources. Ethnic politics was probably the impetus for the division that split the island between North and South. Northerners were seen as chic, world savvy and confident. Southerners as the polar opposite. The northern part of the island was more populous and thus provided a larger tax base for the government because of this density. The south covered a larger area of land and was ignored when it came to essential infrastructure such as utilities and roads. Unfortunately, as a larger part of the Indian population of the island lived from Central Trinidad to its southernmost area the fiscal division was viewed as a racial divide.

***

18. The King's representative

How does a leader make their mark
Upon a savage land
For glory of his King and Monarch
In whose name he doth command

Bringing the rule of law to the brute
'Tis not an easy mission
But my name shall not fall to disrepute
If I play the game of attrition

Pitting one side against the other
Focus on their differences
Blame the other for what they suffer
Through my subtle inferences

Grant my favour to one race
Which? It does not matter
The other feels they are debased
In the chaos, I remain Master

Get them to argue about religion
A whisper here and there
We shall not allow a coalition
To bring ruin to the Empire

Whilst they engage in conflict
Our coffers shall flow over
They will not know that they've been tricked
Or that we are the Controller

The Empire thus shall survive
I say, "God save the King!"
The chaos and hate that we contrive
'Tis stamped with his signet ring.

***

This continued interplay of ethnic identity and political power and the infrastructure dollars that most often go along with that, has given rise to alliances and coalitions that often transcend ideological boundaries. Conflicts and tensions unceasingly simmer beneath the surface of the national discourse. This runs counter to the narrative of a unified nation, and can cause political, racial, and ideological rifts in communities and even families.

The reality is that ethnic politics manifest in the form of political parties and movements that explicitly or implicitly align with ethnic constituencies. This can negatively affect the dynamics of elections, political governance, and policymaking. This in turn influences the distribution of resources, representation, and the articulation of political agendas.

It is important to note however, that ethnic politics can also be positive and is not a singular source of division and discord. While it undeniably shapes the contours of the political landscape, it also serves as a catalyst for collective mobilization and empowerment – as in the case of the Sanathan Dharma Maha Sabha.

Ethnic politics, when harnessed with a spirit of inclusivity and understanding, can become a force for unity and progress, amplifying the voices of marginalized communities and fostering a more equitable society.

Historically however, this has not been the case in Trinidad. That means now is the right time for all citizens to ask themselves:

"How do we reconcile the diversity of our heritage with the unity of our national identity?"

"How do we harness the richness of our cultural tapestry to forge a future that transcends the limitations, hate and violence of the past?"

The twin islands of Trinidad and Tobago are stuck in a dichotomous time loop. To move forward and break the loop, it is critical that the country and its citizenry ask and find answers to these questions.

Ethnic politics has potential to be the true fires in which the aspirations and contradictions of Trinidadian society are forged and smelted. Ideally, it can be a force that both reflects and shapes the collective consciousness. It can be an invitation for Trinidadian society to confront the complexities of the shared history and the possibilities of our shared destiny.

***

19. Lessons Learned

We have learned from the best
We'll put our lesson to the test
A lesson learned from colonial school
It's easiest to divide and rule
Pitting groups against each other
Can cause a person to hate his brother
It's a brilliant colonial trick
To rule the body politic

***

In the shadow of the legacy of colonialism combined with the complexities of our pluralistic society, the dynamics of ethnic politics can serve as a powerful lens through which Trinidadian society can navigate the intricacies of a new unified national identity.

Corruption and Governance

The history of politics in Trinidad and Tobago is marred by the shadows of corruption. Political corruption, like a persistent vine, has coiled its tendrils around the noblest of intentions, strangling the hopes of a nation yearning for true leadership. Consequently, the country has reached a crossroads, where one path will shape the destiny of generations to come in a song of unity and togetherness and the other continues to establish large fracture lines among people that could eventually rip the nation apart.

The primary issue at hand is a systemic one that has twisted and spoiled the political landscape. The insidious nature of corruption, cronyism and nepotism have tainted all levels of governance. This, unchecked, has resulted in a culture of entitlement and malfeasance. The misuse of public funds, the abuse of power, and the erosion of trust have become the hallmark of a system that was meant to serve the people. The problem is clear: corruption in government has become a cancer, threatening to consume the vitality of our nation.

The consequences of ignoring this epidemic are dire indeed. When corruption takes hold, the very soul of a nation is at stake. It sows seeds of distrust among our citizens, engendering a cynicism that corrodes the bonds of community. The impact on our economy is equally devastating, as resources meant for the common good are diverted into the hands of the few. The cost of inaction is immeasurable, for it robs people of their wealth and more insidiously their collective dignity. The rust of corruption eats away at the strength of public trust in the government and its leaders. It is a blight on any public programme and ruinous to any social endeavour.

***

20. Corruption

What government is not at times dishonest
It's the nature of the game
Not delivering what we promised
Is not our source of shame
Absolute power, corrupts absolutely
So, the saying goes
It's all part and parcel of "our duty"
Even for the people who oppose
African, Indian it doesn't matter
We're all playing a grand game
In the end we serve only one master
Would you like to guess its name

***

Yet, even in the face of such daunting odds, there exists a glimmer of hope. The solution lies not in mere rhetoric or empty promises, but in a steadfast commitment to transparency, accountability, and ethical leadership. The solution lies in the hands, minds, and hearts of every citizen. Trinidadians must demand these things of every leader and every party. They must be willing to forgo partisan politics, politics of race and ethnic politics in favour of voting out any corrupt party or leader. This is a guaranteed way to build a governance framework that is impervious to the temptations of corruption, one that serves as a beacon of integrity for all to behold.

To put this solution into action, Trinidadians must first and foremost cultivate a culture of accountability at every level of governance. This demands the creation and independent enforcement of robust anti-corruption laws. This must then be coupled with an independent and vigilant judiciary to ensure their unyielding application. This approach will instill a sense of fairness and impartiality that will most undoubtedly filter down to all levels of society.

Furthermore, transparency must be the watchword of all government and government-related institutions by exposing and purging corrupt elements. Only by upholding these principles can we begin to rebuild the trust that has been so grievously eroded over the decades.

History has shown us the transformative power of integrity in governance. Nations that have successfully confronted the specter of corruption have reaped the rewards of sustained economic growth, social stability, and a renewed sense of national pride. Trinidad and Tobago, too, can aspire to – and achieve - such heights.

A place where the rule of law is not a mere suggestion but an unyielding force that upholds the common good.

This path forward might demand an overhaul of the political system but if the people show their leaders that they will not abide anything less – despite partisan and race politics – then politicians and their political parties will realize that there is no other way.

Trinidad stands at a pivotal juncture, of its history. What kind of Trinidad and Tobago do we wish to bequeath to our children? Will we continue to allow the specter of corruption to cast a long shadow over the future, or will we rise to the challenge and forge a path of integrity and prosperity?

Party Politics = Race Politics

The history of political parties in Trinidad and Tobago is a rich and convoluted one. It is a saga of triumphs and tribulations, of unity and division, and of the perpetual quest for representation and influence. From the days of colonial rule to the present, the evolution of political parties has mirrored the ebb and flow of our nation's collective consciousness.

If we were to trace the origins of political parties in Trinidad and Tobago, we would find ourselves transported back to the nineteenth century, a time when the seeds of dissent and advocacy took root in the hearts of the people. The quest for self-determination and autonomy spurred the formation of the first political organizations, laying the groundwork for the tumultuous journey that lay ahead.

The story of political parties in Trinidad and Tobago is punctuated by moments that have shaped the trajectory of our nation. From the birth of the Trinidadian Labour Party in 1936 to the emergence of the People's National Movement and the United National Congress in the coming decades, each milestone represents a chapter in the ever-evolving narrative of the political landscape. As with any facet of Trinidadian life, the evolution of political parties is influenced by the rich tapestry of the multicultural society, the brutal racism of colonialism and the emergence of an ever-present politics of ethnicity. These forces help form the distinct ideologies of parties rooted in Afro-Trinidadian and Indo-Trinidadian communities.

***

21. Racial Division

If you Black, you must be PNM
'Ain't no if or ands about it
We don't need no CNN
Is true, even if you don't admit it
If you Indian, then you voting UNC

Or some other party ah Indian leading
That is ah ipso facto guarantee
That is truth, is not just a feeling
And if you is ah Indian with the PNM
Then you betraying your race
You ain't no better than anyone ah dem
Dem paying you just to use yuh face
But if you Black and supporting the UNC
You is ah person of great intellect
That is something on which we all agree
A place where me and you could connect
If every time we try to live together
Why must we make it about skin colour
We trying to create a Trinidadian culture
For this to work it must be an "all-in" endeavour
We subject ourselves to the colonial master
Every time we make things about race
Each time we are courting disaster
Each time it is a disgrace
This ridiculous Black on Brown division
Only serves to defeat us all
It is a racist proposition
Inevitably leading to our downfall
Pray my fellow countrymen and women
Let us rise above the racial divide
Race should never put us in opposition
To progress we must leave it behind

***

This distinct separation has had its impact on community interactions. This unavoidably bleeds into Trinidadian politics which has had more than its share of racial challenges and controversies. The tug-of-war for power has often led to impassioned disputes and heated debates, serving as a poignant reminder of the delicate balance between democracy and discord. This inevitably has filtered into the island's social fabric and has continued to cause racial fissures to expand and further drive the island's Afro-Trinidadian and Indo-Trinidadian people apart.

Political parties have learned the lesson of colonialism well. They use the politics of division to stir their base and elicit an "us against them" attitude. This only serves to demonize the "other." In the gap of chaos and discord that is inevitably created, political parties can rule with impunity.

This must change; and the only way to do so is for the people to demand better from their leaders. By choosing to ignore the wedges that are being driven between the races, people can instead force a shift in the conversation, essentially changing the question from "What can you do for Me?" to "What will you do for Us!"

Future of Trinidadian Politics

The infusion of youth and diversity into the political arena, the harnessing of technology for transparent governance, and the nurturing of a culture of accountability and integrity are the pillars upon which a new edifice for a brighter future can be built. The reimagining of policies to embrace the aspirations of all citizens, the empowerment of marginalized voices, and the cultivation of a sense of belonging and ownership can most certainly positively affect the future of the nation. Understandably, these things will not happen overnight. Yet, the seeds of transformation must be sown.

The emergence of grassroots movements that unite the population to clamor for ethical, transparent, and accountable leadership, and the demand for inclusive policies can fuel this revolution. Engaging the voices of the marginalized, the aspirations of the country's youth, and the resilience of the people is the only way to begin the journey.

This can only happen if people shed the colonial mindset. People need to learn to recognize and reject the politics of division and rebuff partisan politics. Instead choosing to reward politicians who, through words and actions, strive for transparency, accountability, and ethics as a fundamental part of their leadership platform.

***

22. All ah we is One

We is one people
For we, colour doesn't matter
All ah we is equal
Dis true now and in de hereafter

We country is no place for disharmony
Don't be here trying to cause division

We people know for a certainty
That will be treated like it is sedition

Allow the people to live as one
Different races, doesn't mean different needs
I guarantee you that in the long run
Dis is how the nation succeeds

***

The future of Trinidadian politics is only part of the narrative in the history of decolonization and self-realization. For Trinidad and Tobago to survive as an independent nation now and into the future, the people must do so in unity. The politics of division may work in larger economies like the United States or Canada, but they quickly run their course in smaller nations. The people will eventually wake up and see how they are being manipulated. This will truly be the beginning of the journey to decolonize the Trinidadian mind.

Decolonizing the Trinidad Mind

Why decolonize the Trinidadian Mind

Trinidad and Tobago, like many nations with a history of colonization, faces the challenge of decolonizing its mindset to foster unity among its diverse population. The negative impacts of colonization linger in the socio-cultural, political, and economic spheres, contributing to growing divisions and disparities. This can lead to an" Us versus Them" mentality which can further lead to increased crime, targeted violence, loss of faith in government and societal breakdown.

Decolonization is a multifaceted process that goes beyond political independence. Breaking away from colonial masters is not enough. It involves recognizing, challenging, and dismantling the enduring impacts of colonization on various aspects of a society, including its culture, education, and social systems. Trinidad, like many other post-colonial nations, continues to grapple with the need to redefine itself beyond the often-invisible constraints imposed by its colonial past.

To address this, the people must develop strategies that promote a shared and unified national identity. This identity must reflect a sense of inclusivity, and collective progress. Thus, we come to where we must propose a way forward. This solution explores various approaches that are all aimed at decolonizing the Trinidad mindset. They focus on different aspect of Trinidadian life and emphasize a need for both government and grassroots initiatives. This must be a very purposeful and strategic approach.

Successful decolonization must begin with the people. There needs to be a critical mass of people of every race who can see the benefit of uniting the nation. Together they can begin the work of dismantling the purposeful barriers that were set between them by the colonizers. That is not just a mindset that must be changed. It must influence every aspect of Trinidadian society; it should affect every interaction between people. This will be no small feat; but it must happen for true decolonization to occur.

Next, government must initiate the work at the macro level, and they must do it without playing partisan or race politics. This will, in turn, empower the community, non-governmental organizations, and social justice organizations to do the same thereby initiating simultaneously a top-down and bottom-up approach that meets in the middle and benefits everyone equally.

Rewriting the History Curricula

One of the primary strategies for decolonizing the Trinidad mind involves reforming the education system. It is important to capture the rich and complex history of the region. However, it is also vitally important to ensure young people understand where they are coming from.

The curriculum should be revised to include a more inclusive and accurate representation of the nation's history. This should emphasize the contributions of all ethnic and cultural groups. Revising the national history curriculum to include perspectives and contributions of indigenous peoples, African slaves, Indian indentured laborers, and other marginalized groups is crucial. This may involve creating new textbooks and educational materials that emphasize the richness and diversity of Trinidad and Tobago's history.

This can help challenge stereotypes, correct historical inaccuracies, and promote a more nuanced understanding of Trinidad and Tobago's rich heritage. In addition to content, the education system should also focus on fostering critical thinking, empathy, and intercultural understanding. Schools can implement extra-curricular programs that encourage students to learn about and appreciate the diverse backgrounds of their peers. Cultural exchange programs, language courses, and collaborative projects can create opportunities for students to interact with different communities. This approach can break down barriers and foster a sense of unity.

***

23. The Schoolbag

The future of the nation lies
In the schoolbags of our children
This was true in the past
Just as much as it is true in the present

We must ensure our children
Have a better chance than their parents
Or all we would have eventually done
Is create a group of antisocial dilettantes
If they can see nothing to strive for
Or cannot picture a future bright
Then as a nation we've failed them
And robbed them of their birthright

***

Trinidad and Tobago, like many former colonies, bears the scars of colonization in its education system. Decolonizing the Trinidadian mind involves dismantling the structures and ideologies rooted in colonialism to foster a more inclusive, culturally relevant, and empowering education.

Figure 13 – "The future of the nation is in the bookbag of our children" Dr. Eric Williams

It is essential to find areas of focus in education that could help decolonize the Trinidadian mind. These elements are conceived to build upon each other; for example, a curriculum overhaul ideally should include cultural enrichment through culture sharing, language revitalization, a revision of the selected text uses to pass on the history of pre- and post-colonization and so on.

Curriculum Overhaul

One of the fundamental steps in decolonizing education is re-evaluating and restructuring the curriculum. It is fantastic that the current curriculum reflects a Caribbean geo-political perspective. This helps students see the larger picture and how Trinidad fits into it. However, it cannot be done at the expense of sidelining the histories and legacy of the African enslaved and the heritage of the East Indian indentured labourers.

A more inclusive curriculum could incorporate the diverse cultural and historical experiences of Trinidad and Tobago. Exploring the origins of innovators and thinkers of every race, religion and political stripe will help open young minds. Discussing the positive and negative impacts with the benefit of hindsight, will help critical thinking. This approach would give students a more comprehensive understanding and a deeper appreciation of their identity and heritage.

Furthermore, learning about the other cultures within the Trinidadian milieu would help them be more understanding and empathetic of their fellow students. Often such radical change as a curriculum overhaul, is best done in stages and any one of the following elements would be a good start. The concept of "low hanging fruit" would help to identify the easiest path to initiate the change process.

Incorporating Cultural Knowledge

In Canada, the British used residential schools as a tool to "tame the Indian." The purpose of these schools was to separate the Indigenous children from their culture. In doing so, they could be moulded into whatever the colonial masters wanted them to be.

Separating people from their cultural origins has a deleterious effect on the person and their society. Lost in the wilderness of not belonging, they are unable to contribute to a society and social structures. Indeed, why contribute to a society that perpetrated such violence to the person, their culture and race?

Highlighting and incorporating racial and cultural knowledge into the educational framework is crucial for decolonization. This involves recognizing and respecting the wealth of knowledge embedded in local traditions, languages, and practices. This does not only hold true for East Indian culture for inasmuch as many might want to deny it the enslaved Africans also had their own rich local traditions, and powerful cultural norms.

By integrating these racialized perspectives into various subjects, students would be encouraged to develop a more nuanced understanding of their cultural context.

Cultural Exchange Programs

Promoting cultural exchange programs within the Caribbean and beyond can expose students to a variety of perspectives and worldviews. Experiencing different cultures firsthand fosters a sense of global citizenship while also reinforcing the importance of local identity. Such programs can be instrumental in breaking down stereotypes and fostering cross-cultural understanding.

Community Involvement

Decolonization is not solely the responsibility of educational institutions. Engaging the local community in the education process is essential. Community leaders, elders, and experts can contribute valuable insights, ensuring that the education system is not isolated from the lived experiences and needs of the people it serves.

Critical Thinking and Media Literacy

Encouraging critical thinking skills and media literacy is crucial for decolonizing the Trinidadian mind. Students should be equipped to analyze information critically, question narratives, and recognize biases. This empowers them to navigate the complex sociopolitical landscape with a discerning eye and a more informed perspective.

Decolonizing the Trinidadian mind through educational reforms is a multidimensional process that requires commitment, collaboration, and a deep understanding of the local context. By reimagining the education system to be more inclusive, reflective of local knowledge, and culturally diverse, Trinidad and Tobago can pave the way for a generation with a liberated and decolonized mindset, which would be poised to contribute meaningfully to a more equitable society.

Cultural Preservation and Promotion

Trinidad's cultural diversity is a unique strength that can be harnessed for national unity. Efforts to preserve and promote diverse cultural expressions, including music, dance, art, and language, can contribute to a more inclusive national identity. Cultural festivals, exhibitions, and public events that celebrate the nation's diversity can become platforms for fostering understanding and appreciation among different communities.

***

24. We ting

Carnival, is we ting
Is we time to break away
Get rid of all the stress
In a three-day ramajay[6]

This is the biggest party in the world
People coming from all over
We come here to get on bad
We come here to takeover

Sita Ram[7] my brother and sister
Happy Diwali[8] to you and yours
The light of the diya[9] will be your guide
May Mother Lakshmi[10] remove your fears

My friend Asaalam alaykum[11]
Though we may not always get along
I will surely wish you the best
For together is how we become strong

---

[6] A colloquial word for party

[7] A Hindu greeting
[8] Hindu festival of lights
[9] A small clay pot used to light a wick
[10] Hindu Goddess of Light
[11] Islamic greeting meaning Peace be unto you

***

Government support for cultural initiatives is crucial. Establishing cultural centers, providing funding for community-based projects, and incorporating diverse cultural events into national celebrations can highlight the richness of Trinidad's heritage. By embracing and celebrating all aspects of the nation's culture, citizens are more likely to feel a sense of belonging and pride in their shared identity.

Cultural Preservation as Resistance

Preserving our culture and traditions is an act of resistance against the erasure of identity imposed by colonization. Trinidad's cultural diversity, stemming from African, Indian, and Indigenous influences, creates a vibrant mosaic that deserves protection. Efforts to preserve traditional practices, languages, rituals, and art forms serve as a tangible assertion of Trinidad's autonomy.

***

25. A Cultural Journey

TnT is the land of the steel pan
But friend it's more than that by far
Our history is rich and complex
So please allow me to share
First let us start with our beaches
From the North, South, East and West
Their splendour is unexplainable
Though many have tried their best
From Icacos to Maracas
Quinam and Mayaro
Our island beaches promise
To wash away your sorrow
Don't forget Tobago's beaches
With sand and sun delights
Where many a happy tourist
Dance away the night
Nylon Pool and Bucco Reef
Just one of many charms
Wondrous nature's majesty
Under the Caribbean stars
Our food is simply delicious
Whether Creole or East Indian
Not just tasty but nutritious
The talk of the Caribbean
Fruits like mango, chennet and plum

And oh, so many more
For sure your taste buds will succumb
If you take time to explore

Figure 14 - Aspects of Trinidadian Culture and Geography

***

26. Diasporic Regrets

My mother told me the story of Rama
When I was still a child
I am sure that knowing I still remember
Might have made her smile

I learned Artha, Kama, Moksha, and Dharma
Growing up into my teens
She taught me about the rules of karma
And everything in between

But the one thing I did not learn
Was the Hindi language
Now in my later years I yearn
For that singular advantage

I did not know that my mother tongue
Would give me a sense of belonging
Ah the ignorance of the young
Often fills one's life with longing

***

Museums and Archives as Guardians of History

Museums and archives play a pivotal role in preserving and displaying Trinidad's history. By curating exhibits that highlight the pre-colonial, colonial, and post-colonial eras, these institutions contribute to a nuanced understanding of Trinidad's past. The inclusion of diverse narratives, voices, and perspectives helps challenge the Eurocentric viewpoints that often dominate historical discourse.

There is a place for all types of museums that capture the historical, social, political, and religious heart and soul of the island.

These treasured places that need to become part of the national discourse; from the Mud House Museum in Avocat to the National Museum, the Indian Caribbean Museum to Fort George. This can only happen with government intervention with a systematic and concerted effort to highlight and raise awareness of these historical places. This should be done through multi-ministerial coordination including the Ministries of Community Development, Culture and the Arts, Education, Social Services, Public Administration and Communications and Tourism.

Cultural Promotion for Inclusivity

Cultural promotion is equally crucial for decolonization. It involves actively celebrating and integrating diverse cultures into mainstream society. Festivals, cultural events, and public initiatives that showcase Trinidad's unique blend of traditions create a more inclusive national narrative. The message needs to be loud and clear – these are not Indian, Black, Hindu, or Muslim events. They are Trinidadian cultural events. Losing these identity markers within the larger social context will help in building bridges and greater cross-racial participation.

By highlighting the contributions of different communities, these efforts counteract the marginalization often perpetuated by colonial legacies. These activities, however, cannot be done within a cultural vacuum and every attempt must be made to ensure that the atmosphere and opportunities exist for cross-cultural to occur. Although the Best Village and Mastana Bahar competitions are examples of this cross-cultural participation should be encouraged.

Community Engagement and Empowerment:

Decolonization is not a top-down process; it requires active participation from communities. Empowering local communities to take charge of their cultural narratives fosters a sense of ownership and agency. Grassroots initiatives, community-led projects, and partnerships between cultural organizations can amplify the voices of Trinidad's diverse population.

Inclusive Policies and Governance

Decolonizing the Trinidad mindset requires a commitment to inclusive governance and policies that address historical inequalities. The reason the colonial masters used the trick of dividing to rule in their colonies was because it worked. For the East Indians it was pitting those with fair skin against their dark skin compatriots. Later was it was pitting Muslim against Hindu. In Trinidad it was the Black people against the newly arrived East Indian indentured labourers.

Unfortunately, the hate and distrust between the races continues to this day. What's worse is that even in a post-colonial Trinidad and Tobago, that hate, and distrust is still being used by many people to further their own agendas.

Inclusive policies must be designed to uplift marginalized groups, including those who have historically been disadvantaged due to factors such as race, ethnicity, and socioeconomic status. This could involve targeted initiatives for small and medium enterprises within marginalized communities, as well as educational and vocational programs to enhance skill development and employment opportunities.

Trinidad boasts a rich tapestry of cultures, shaped by the contributions of indigenous peoples, Africans, Indians, Chinese, Europeans, and others. However, colonial legacies have sometimes led to the marginalization of certain cultural expressions. Inclusive policies should celebrate and preserve the diverse cultural heritage of Trinidad, ensuring that all communities feel a sense of pride and belonging. This could involve supporting cultural events, festivals, and initiatives that highlight the contributions of various ethnic and cultural groups.

Education plays a pivotal role in decolonization, as it shapes perceptions, values, and societal norms. An inclusive education system in Trinidad should reflect the nation's diverse history, emphasizing the contributions of all communities. This involves revising curricula to be more representative, promoting cultural sensitivity, and fostering an environment where students from diverse backgrounds feel valued and included.

Inclusive governance requires equitable political representation, ensuring that all voices are heard in decision-making processes. Affirmative action policies can be implemented to increase the representation of underrepresented groups in political institutions.

Media Representation and Narrative

The media plays a powerful role in shaping public perceptions and reinforcing cultural stereotypes. To decolonize the Trinidad mindset, there must be a concerted effort to challenge and change prevailing narratives. This involves promoting diverse voices in media, ensuring accurate representation of all communities, and dismantling harmful stereotypes.

Government support for media diversity initiatives, including subsidies for independent media outlets that represent different perspectives, can contribute to a more inclusive media landscape.

Media literacy programs in schools and communities can empower individuals to critically engage with the media, fostering a more discerning and informed citizenry.

Grassroots Initiatives and Civic

Engagement

While government-led initiatives are essential, grassroots movements and civil society organizations also play a crucial role in decolonizing the Trinidad mindset. Community-based projects that promote dialogue, understanding, and collaboration among diverse groups can contribute to unity at the local level. Initiatives that address social issues, such as poverty and inequality, from a collaborative perspective can build solidarity among communities.

Civil society organizations can also serve as advocates for inclusive policies and social justice. By mobilizing communities and raising awareness about the impacts of colonization, these organizations can create a groundswell of support for decolonization efforts. Collaborative projects between different communities, facilitated by grassroots organizations, can demonstrate the shared interests and common goals that unite Trinidad and Tobago.

Community Policing and Crime

Prevention

Trinidad and Tobago face significant challenges related to the rise of crime and the efficacy of its policing efforts. While this is not a book about policing and judicial reforms that need to take place, there are some high-level conversations that must happen.

Firstly, it must be acknowledged that this is a highly complex multidimensional problem. Secondly it demands input from various ministries within the government and probably assistance from external countries. Finally, we must remember that society at large has an equally important role to play.

There is a concept called criminal escalation. This is an understanding that people involved in crime often progress from less serious offenses to more severe ones over time. Researchers believe that criminal behavior often escalates due to specific factors and influences that build up gradually, leading individuals to commit increasingly serious crimes. It suggests that people rarely start with serious crimes but may progress to them.

This process can involve a combination of personal choices and external influences. There are environmental influences where people are exposed to crime-ridden environments may become desensitized to criminal behavior. Another might be peer pressure where friends or associates who engage in crime can lead others down a similar path. Undoubtedly addiction or substance abuse can lead people to commit increasingly serious crimes, either to support the habit or while under its influence. There are situations of dire financial need where economic pressures can lead someone to start with minor theft and then escalate as their needs grow or circumstances worsen. Finally, there are psychological factors where dome may seek thrills or are driven by unmet needs for power, recognition, or control.

Generally, it is accepted that many of these situations early intervention is key. Community programs and positive role models can redirect at-risk youth. The government must also directly address root causes such as issues like poverty, addiction, and education all of which can reduce the risk of escalation. There must also be a level of personal responsibility where the citizen must accept a level of personal accountability.

Criminal escalation is a progressive process that can pull people from minor infractions into serious criminal acts. By understanding why it happens and identifying factors that contribute to it, society can better prevent this cycle and encourage positive change.

Government	**Law Enforcement**	**Public**
Strengthen the legal and justice System	Promote public trust through transparency and accountability	Complain or Compliment
Invest in law enforcement including technological advancements where applicable	Adopt a zero-tolerance approach to law enforcement	Community Engagement
Promote public trust through transparency and accountability	Address compliments and complaints	Brother's Keeper

Government	Law Enforcement	Public
Adopt a zero-tolerance approach to crimes and misdemeanours	Community Engagement and Participation	Individual responsibility
Address compliments and complaints		

Government Commitment and Funding

The government of Trinidad and Tobago must prioritize addressing the rise of crime by allocating sufficient financial resources to law enforcement agencies. This includes funding for infrastructure upgrades, technology investments, personnel training, and community policing initiatives. Additionally, sustained commitment from policymakers is essential to ensure that anti-crime efforts remain a top priority in national agendas.

Legislative Reforms

To effectively combat crime, Trinidad and Tobago should consider enacting legislative reforms that strengthen the legal framework governing law enforcement activities. This may include updating existing laws to better address emerging forms of criminal activity, enhancing penalties for serious offenses, and streamlining judicial processes to expedite the prosecution of criminals.

Collaboration with International Partners
Given the transnational nature of many criminal activities, Trinidad and Tobago should actively engage with international partners, including neighboring countries, regional organizations, and global law enforcement agencies. Collaboration on intelligence-sharing, joint operations, and capacity-building initiatives can enhance the effectiveness of anti-crime efforts and facilitate the apprehension of criminals operating across borders.

Public Awareness and Education Campaigns

Public engagement and cooperation are crucial components of successful crime prevention strategies. Therefore, the government should launch comprehensive public awareness campaigns to educate citizens about crime risks, prevention measures, and the importance of community involvement in law enforcement efforts. By fostering a culture of vigilance and civic responsibility, Trinidad and Tobago can empower its population to play an active role in combating crime.

Trinidad and Tobago face formidable challenges stemming from the rise of crime and the limitations of its current policing infrastructure. However, by implementing strategic infrastructural changes and enacting supportive policies, the country can enhance its law enforcement capabilities and mitigate the threats posed by criminal activities. It is imperative for the government, law enforcement agencies, civil society organizations, and international partners to collaborate closely and remain committed to the shared goal of ensuring the safety and security of all citizens. Through concerted efforts and sustained investments in crime prevention and policing, Trinidad and Tobago can build a safer and more prosperous future for its people.

Conclusion

One of the primary strategies for decolonizing the Decolonizing the Trinidad mindset is a multifaceted and ongoing process that requires concerted efforts from both the government and grassroots initiatives. Educational reforms, cultural preservation, inclusive policies, media representation, and community engagement are all essential components of a comprehensive strategy.

By addressing the historical legacies of colonization, fostering a sense of shared national identity, and promoting inclusivity, Trinidad and Tobago can pave the way for a more united and harmonious future. The journey towards decolonization is not without challenges, but the potential benefits for social cohesion, economic development, and national pride make it a worthy endeavor for the people and the government alike.

27. The Call of the Kiskadee

Figure 15 by Unknown Author

Wandering amid
Fevered dreams
Of endless beaches
Dried up streams
A mysterious sound
Breaks through
The reverie
A melodic call arises
The kiskadee rings in
The morning air
Calls of

Kis kis ki dee
Here I stand surrounded by
Sun blasted plants and people
Rays burning in to our
Collective bodies
Cooking up ideas that bubble
To the surface
Then disappear
An endless stream of
Vehicular traffic
Monotonous
Gaseous
Fumes
Assaulting senses
Kis kis ki dee
Sings the
Vivacious avian
Bring me back to reality
The sun has toasted me
Roasted me
Inside out
Oh lord I'm hot
The floor is lava and
Heat above
And
Below
But we endure

Me and
My fellow Trinidadians
Kis kis ki dee
She sings in her open-air aviary
Coconuts on the tree
Screaming pick me pick me
I can cool you down
They yield their
Thirst repelling juice to the
Coconut man's blade
Rushing into my mouth
Running down my
Arms
As I anticipate the luscious jelly
Hiding within its
Hardened skull
Kis kis ki dee
Sings the bird up in
Her tree
Sights and sounds
Colours and smells
Taunts the senses and
Stirs them well
Memories of a
Bygone time
Making new memories
And feeding new

Rhymes
Fruits and vegetables
Duck and goat
Fresh fish
Bought from the man
Right off
The boat
Overwhelmed taste buds
Crying in delight
Over filled bellies
Late in the night
Kis kis ki dee
Our feathered friend sings
As she takes once
To the wing
This is Trinidad
Jewel of the Caribbean
Standing tall to the
Burning sun
Concrete jungle
Wave lapped beaches
Verdant jungles
A lake of pitch but
Rocky roads still
Rough and tumble
Riddim section
Pulsing beats

Bodies writhing
With the
Tassa's heat
Accompanied by
Our feathered friend
Kis kis kid dee
From the island's
Southern beaches to the
Mountainous
Northern range
Surrounded by
A burglar proof jail
Bandits in the night
Prevail
Kis kis ki dee
Beauty
Violence
Music and
Dance
The island's
Dichotomy
Filled with contrast
Haunting melody
Calling the diaspora
In sultry tones
Come back babies
Come back home

Kis kis ki dee
Kis kis ki dee

Index

Glossary

WORD	MEANING
Tabla	An East Indian drum
Dat	Slang for the word That
Ah	Slang for the word I
Shadeism	Shadeism or colourism is prejudice based on skin tone. It is usually associated with a marked preference for lighter-skinned people
Prabhu	Literally translated to master or prince in Sanskrit. It is also a name sometimes applied to God
Gangplank	A movable plank used as a ramp to board or disembark from a ship or boat
TrinBagonian	An inhabitant of Trinidad and Tobago or a person of Trinidadian or Tobagonian descent
Rupees	The basic monetary unit of India, Pakistan, Sri Lanka, Nepal, Mauritius, and the Seychelles

WORD	**MEANING**
Chutney	A spicy condiment made of fruits or vegetables with vinegar, spices, and sugar, originating in India
Ghee	Clarified butter made from the milk of a buffalo or cow, used in South Asian cooking
Lord Shiva	Shiva is a prominent god of Hinduism. His name means "Auspicious One," and he is a member of the trinity of supreme gods
Naam kya hai	Hindi for "What is your name?"
Dalit	A member of the lowest class in the traditional Hindu social hierarchy. Dalits were also formerly referred to as untouchables, a term that is now understood to be offensive
Hindustan	Traditionally northern India and meaning the 'Land of the Hindus'
Doubles	Doubles is a common street food originating in Trinidad and Tobago. It consists of curried chickpeas served on two fried flatbreads

WORD	MEANING
Saltfish buljol	Saltfish buljol is a salad dish of the cuisine of Trinidad and Tobago. It consists of chopped salted cod, tomatoes, and chilies. The name is of French origin
Oil down	Oil down is a stew of breadfruit, salted meat, chicken, dumplings, callaloo, and other vegetables stewed in coconut milk, herbs, and spices
Souse	Souse, a light Caribbean dish, served cold, that traditionally consists of pickled pig meat in a clear broth flavoured with seasonings
Hosay	The Hosay or Husay (derived from Husayn or Hussein) commemoration is a Caribbean manifestation of the Shia Muslim Remembrance of Muharram in Trinidad and Tobago
Cascadura fish	An armored catfish of the family Callichthyidaehe. The other name for this delicacy is "cascadura."

WORD	MEANING
Massa	A spoken alliteration of the word Master
Dem	Slang word for Them
Ramajay	Ramajay generally means to sing and make music
Sita Ram	An Indian greeting
Diwali	Diwali is one of the major religious festivals in Hinduism. The festival generally symbolizes the victory of light over darkness
Mother Lakshmi	Hindu goddess of wealth, good fortune, happiness, youth, and beauty
Asaalam alaykum	A greeting that means ' Peace be upon you'
Kiskadee	The Great Kiskadee (so named for its three-syllable call) is one of the largest and most boisterous members of the tyrant flycatcher family
Tassa	Refers to a drumming ensemble drawn from an amalgamation of various North Indian folk drumming traditions

Index

[i] https://caribbeanhistoryarchives.blogspot.com/2018/12/sweet-sorrow-timeline-of-sugar-in.html
[ii] https://westindiandiplomacy.com/indian-indentured-labourers-in-trinidad/
[iii] https://www.britannica.com/topic/transatlantic-slave-trade/The-Middle-Passage
[iv] https://www.britannica.com/biography/C-L-R-James
[v] https://www.thoughtco.com/toussaint-louverture-4135900
[vi] https://www.rmg.co.uk/stories/blog/nanny-maroons
[vii] https://enslaved.org/fullStory/16-23-126818/
[viii] Kala Pani taboo - https://en.wikipedia.org/wiki/Kala_pani_(taboo)#:~:text=The%20kala%20pani%20(lit.,one's%20cultural%20character%20and%20posterity.
[ix] Cipriani, Arthur Andrew - https://www.encyclopedia.com/humanities/encyclopedias-almanacs-transcripts-and-maps/cipriani-arthur-andrew-1878-1945
[x] Tubal Uriah "Buzz" Butler: Man of the People - https://nationaltrust.tt/home/butler-man-of-the-people/?v=df1f3edb9115
[xi] Rudranath Capildeo - https://en.wikipedia.org/wiki/Rudranath_Capildeo
[xii] Eric Williams - https://www.britannica.com/biography/Eric-Williams

www.ingramcontent.com/pod-product-compliance
Lightning Source LLC
Chambersburg PA
CBHW051835090426
42736CB00011B/1819
* 9 7 8 1 7 3 8 0 4 1 9 8 5 *